Guerrilla Warfare for Business:

Fight to Survive and Grow in Small Business

by Dimitri Livas

Copyright 2018 by Dimitri Livas

All rights reserved

ISBN-13: 978-0-9876338-0-4

No part of this book may be reproduced in any form or by any electronic or mechanical means, including information storage and retrieval systems, without written permission from the author, except for the use of brief quotations in a book review.

Although every precaution has been taken to verify the accuracy of the information contained herein, the author and publisher assume no responsibility for any errors or omissions. No liability is assumed for damages that may result from the use of information contained within.

Table of Contents

Dedication iv

INTRODUCTION 1

Chapter 1 - F: FREEDOM....................................15

Chapter 2 - I: INSPIRE 34

Chapter 3 - G: GROW 57

Chapter 4 - H: HERO..78

Chapter 5 - T: TRUTH (and Authenticity) 94

CONCLUSION 112

Dedication

To Nada for your continued support and confidence in the roller coaster of uncertainty that I have taken us on in this life of small business. Thank you for believing in me and never losing hope.

To Natasha, my little warrior who never gives up, I'm so proud of you. Keep using that endless energy to fight the right way in life; keep questioning, learning and discovering; and, most of all, keep that creative spirit alive.

To Hanna, you're such an incredible and talented girl, you can do anything you set your mind too with your shining smile and caring nature. Never stop reaching for your dreams, and if you ever stumble along the way, dust yourself off and keep pushing forward.

INTRODUCTION

To have any chance of succeeding as a start-up or small business against all the giant entrenched corporations, you have to fight. There's no room for passivity, for blind faith, for just hoping it will all work out and be okay. You fight for every contract, every sale, every connection, every scrap.

Why do we need to have this fighter's spirit, this mindset? According to the Australian Bureau of Statistics, a whopping 60% of small businesses fail in their first three years.

I believe you have to have the right mindset — and it's a fighter's mindset. But it's not about aggression or physical violence, as you'll learn.

This book is focused on the unique challenges we face in small and medium-sized business. Usually, a small business starts out as one person's dream, but that initial dream can get swallowed up by the immense odds that keep getting stacked against us.

There's a way through, a way to succeed. Sometimes, it's a practical battle; sometimes, it's one within us. Usually, it's a combination of the two.

The focus of this book is on your mindset: essentially, how to develop it for success. I'll share with you the real-world lessons I've learnt to survive and grow my own successful businesses, and I'll talk you through the steps you can take to develop the mental agility and personal resilience to succeed in your own business.

We need to constantly innovate and motivate ourselves to keep going, keeping our eyes open. We need to adapt to survive, and it takes endurance. At the same time, we need to recognise our advantages. Small businesses can respond quicker to changing circumstances, especially in niche markets. We can steer our speedboat quickly, while corporations lumber forward like the Titanic.

However, traditional methods are also not enough. Open any textbook, or look at the content of an academic business course, and you'll find great ideas and proven advice: get inspired by a great idea, raise some capital, lease premises, and hire staff to produce and sell your idea, create a marketing department, saturate social media and billboards with your brand for a year, buy radio advertising, create TV ads, employ a sales team, and so on... all useful, effective stuff — that requires a substantial budget. There'll be time and money for that further down the road.

So, what about now, right now? What are the most practical, straightforward, valuable, and cost-effective hacks you can employ to keep your business alive, and to give your business the best chance of success? You'll find them in the pages of this book — all based on real-world lessons I've learnt from a lifetime in business.

Whether you're a start-up or an established business looking to expand into a new market, your resources and budgets are almost always limited, and you'll nearly always be competing with established players and large corporations with huge budgets. If you attempt to go at it toe to toe, simply: you'll lose.

You'll lose in a war of attrition, and you will have spent more money than what comes back in. You'll get swallowed up and die. Take Ralph Sarich's remarkable orbital engine, which promised to revolutionise car manufacturing and reduce petrol consumption. His larger, Titanic competitors bought him out and shelved the idea. Why? So they could continue building the inefficient (but lucrative) car designs they had always built.

You have to be innovative and clever as a start-up. You have to use your resources wisely for maximum impact and maximum effect.

You need to think differently and fight differently.

You need to use guerrilla warfare strategies and tactics that work in the real world.

Why guerrilla warfare?

Because business, all business, has to be built on grit, determination, resilience, and the adaptability to survive. When you've learnt how to survive — only then can you grow and thrive.

I'd like to share a mantra with you that I lived by virtually my entire life:

Guerrilla Warfare for Business

If you fight, you might lose, but if you don't fight, you've already lost.

When it comes to defending nations and land, guerrilla tactics have been around for centuries. They're usually the domain of the underdog, the smaller armies or resurgence groups who don't have the weaponry, training, and numbers to fight like-for-like on the battlefield.

Here's a story that illustrates this perfectly. In the 14th Century, a group of peasants in Morgarten, Switzerland, defended their land from the Austrian army. The Austrian army, 20,000 men strong, far outnumbered the Swiss civilians who were a mere 2,000 in number.

Still, the Swiss defended their land: ambushing the soldiers and forcing them down a narrow path between a steep slope and a swamp. Using the tactical and strategic advantage of higher ground, the peasants hurled long-handled axes and even logs and rocks at their opponents, defeating them with ease.

Now, I'm not for one moment suggesting you start fashioning a long-handled axe or reaching for the nearest rock — but just think about the simple ingenuity of those men and their plan, not to mention the sheer will and determination to fight for what was important to them. They created the circumstances for a win. They thought — *or fought* — outside of the box, and it paid off.

I've always been inspired by those who use what they have to maximum effect and aren't afraid to fight — in a metaphorical sense — a little differently, and history is full of examples of guerrilla warfare being used to great effect.

Their common features are:

A government, often corrupt, that has lost the support of its people.

A struggle, usually on a "David and Goliath" scale.

An "evil empire" – this may be the government itself, or an external force.

In business terms, think of a "corrupt government" as a market rival, the people as customers and an "evil empire" as a major opposing corporation.

Guerrilla Warfare for Business

So where do you fit in as a small business? Well, if we go with the David and Goliath set-up, you're David. Your gargantuan opponents might appear stronger, but a well-timed and well-placed retaliation can and will turn your situation around.

One of the most famous examples of guerrilla warfare in history would have to be Francis Marion's campaigns against the British during the American Revolutionary War. He earned the moniker "Swamp Fox" when British Colonel Banastre Tarleton, after unsuccessfully pursuing Marion through 26 miles of swamp, gave up and swore, "For this damned old fox, the devil himself could not catch him." Because of his cunning, expert and skill in guerrilla warfare, he was appointed a brigadier general.

So, how do you use what you have to develop your own guerrilla strategies for successful business?

It's back to mindset. If you follow the five fighters' steps outlined in this book, you'll develop the mindset that will enable your business to survive and grow.

It's about fighting the right way to win every day.

It's about arming your people and sharpening the three key weapons for success, those practical tools that will:

- Increase revenue

- Reduce costs

- Grow your market share

And it's about creating a vision to lead and inspire your people to come on that journey with you, and teaching them the skills to build them into the fighters you need on your team.

Why listen to me?

I've started a number of successful businesses in the past twenty years, and all have had their share of highs and lows. Each one has gone to hell at some point… and then made the journey back.

I've been through the fire and survived to achieve repeated victories, so I'm superconfident about creating sustainable success in business. Business gets me excited; helping people gets me excited. One of the privileges of weathering so many storms and learning the lessons I've learned comes in passing those lessons on — whether I'm delivering a keynote speech, facilitating ideas in the workshops I run, providing fresh insights at the presentations I'm invited to give, or on the pages of this book you're reading right now.

You see, I've always been a fighter in some way or another, but for many years, I only knew one way to fight. And although it laid the foundations for fighting to win, to keep my place, to survive, there was a better way.

Picture this: I'm walking through a huge set of iron gates for the first time. They close and lock behind me. I've never been through these gates before; I'm excited and, despite my naturally friendly nature, I'm also a little apprehensive because through those gates, I'm greeted by a bunch of unfamiliar faces.

I do what you do in these situations, and what comes easy to me: I smile.

No one smiles back.

So, I smile bigger.

Still, no one smiles back. Then this guy — I found out later he was called Greg — does something.

Greg lifts his arm and he points a finger at me, inches from my face.

I have no idea why. Then he says something. He says this one word, a word which at this time in my life I have never heard before, but a word that will become a hair trigger for me for years to come.

He points at me, screws up his face as if in some sort of pain, and says, "Wog", and not just once. He keeps saying it in a rhythm, and others join in, following Greg's lead, pointing and chanting the word *Wog* over and over, louder and louder.

With my back to the locked gates and nowhere to run, the crowd closes in. I feel threatened and in danger, and I just want to get out of this situation — but I'm stuck. I finally snap, and, with a flurry of punches that have more emotion than technique, I pummel Greg to the ground.

When do you think this event occurred? First day of college? High School maybe?

No. I was five years old, and this was my first day at Kindergarten.

Suddenly, the reality of it hit me and tears flowed. I looked back to where my dad had dropped me off, just outside those big, iron gates — but he'd already driven away in his yellow Ford Falcon, oblivious to what had just happened to his youngest boy.

This was the last time my dad would drive me to school, and in fact, it was one of the last times I'd ever see him again; he died in a horrific car crash just a few weeks after.

Having attained the status of Heavyweight Champion of the Kindergarten sandbox, I learnt throughout my schooling that using my fists was the way to deal with bullies, because the teachers sure as hell didn't help — unless you count that ineffective piece of advice of being told "to just ignore it." That was too passive for me — I preferred my mantra: "If you fight, you might lose; if you don't fight, you've already lost."

Now, it didn't end there. Fast forward ten years and by the age of fifteen the taunts got a bit more narky. One clever guy named Ken managed to mix taunts about my dad's death together with the wog and greaser insults.

So, after he and his mates held me down and beat me up one day behind the school gym, and I was lying there bleeding and bruised, humiliated and hurt, the mantra came into my mind. I jumped up, fought my heart out and almost killed him — nearly sending myself to jail, but achieving my dream of being able to go to school without fear any more.

Fast forward another ten years. I'm now 25, I've completed a degree in commerce, run a couple of successful businesses, started dabbling in construction and have a wonderful fiancé. But I still have this mantra in my head: and this idea that showing my strength can only happen with my fists.

So, when I get into an argument with a guy in an outdoor restaurant in the middle of the day, and he decides it would be a good idea to throw a bread roll at my head, I hurl him across some tables. All because he threw a bread roll at my head.

Needless to say, my friends were shocked and not overly impressed. It was a wake-up call for me, time to rethink my whole attitude to life and success.

I decided to change, to retrain myself, and I realised I could adapt that mantra, "If you fight, you might lose; if you don't fight, you've already lost," by applying it metaphorically. I studied, learnt and practiced negotiation skills, sales, persuasion, and business skills, I found people who had perfected and used these skills to learn from, so that I could direct the fight in ways that would improve my life.

The mantra has become one of my pillars of strength, because I believe that it's only when we stop fighting, when we settle, when we give in and give up to a stronger force that we lose.

It's a matter of fighting the right way, of learning the right skills, to manoeuvre to survive and to grow our strength so that we can live a fulfilling life — on our own terms.

So now, almost 40 years on from that Kindergarten fight, I'm still fighting. I have two children, two beautiful girls aged ten and six, and a wonderful wife who's been with me since we were eighteen, and they're the reason I keep fighting: skilling myself to be the best role model I can be for my kids.

Outside of the daily thrills and pressures of running several successful businesses, I've added presenting and professional speaking to my skillset — skills I've had a blast honing and playing around with. I get to speak about what I love — how lucky am I? I collected and distilled the lessons I've learnt to inspire and coach others. Putting all of that into this book was the next natural progression for me.

So look at that mantra once more and keep it in mind as you journey through the book, applying it to your business, your life, and your living.

If you fight, you might lose, but if you don't fight, you've already lost.

Chapter 1 -
F: FREEDOM

So, here's a question for you:

Can you control your life?

Or is life, for the most part, simply out of our control?

Does life happen to us, or do we create it?

Or, is there something bigger at play? Does someone else create our destiny?

My ancestors, the ancient Greeks believed in the Moirai, a group of three weaving goddesses who assign individual destinies to us mere mortals at birth. In English they're known as the Fates.

Whether you buy into that or not, you'll still find softer versions of these beliefs in today's world. When something goes wrong in your life, you might hear the line, "Everything happens for a reason," as a way to placate you, or soften the blow.

Here's what I think: if we choose to believe that we walk a predestined path, then we're accepting that it's incredibly hard for us to escape fate or change the life we've been assigned.

Sure, we can steer the ship, so to speak. Every day, we try to direct the course of our life by making choices around health, work, and finances.

But really, are our efforts futile? Doesn't life do whatever the hell it wants? Does life give a damn what you or I think?

Security, stability, and control: are these just well-crafted illusions? After all, you'll get sick. Eventually you'll lose loved ones and you'll suffer, and you'll get old and your body will get stiff… so what's the point in even trying to control what we ultimately have no power over?

Well, let me tell you a story about a man who made a choice. A man who was kept in captivity in appalling conditions. A man who was ultimately freed but by then had lost everything dear to his heart.

And yet.

And yet he still showed the world that no matter what we experience, no matter what situations life puts us in — we still have choice.

Why? How?

Because we have the power to choose, the power to create, the power to shape our destiny, and the power to grow and to truly be free.

His name was Viktor Frankl

In the thick of World War II, Viktor Frankl, an Austrian doctor, was arrested, along with his parents, his wife, and his brother. All five were sent to a Nazi concentration camp. Frankl's father died within six months.

Over the course of the following three years, Frankl was separated from his loved ones and moved between four different concentration camps, including the infamous Auschwitz. When he was finally liberated in 1945, he learned the terrible news that his wife, his brother and his mother had all been killed during their time in the death camps.

Frankl's experience and skill in psychology had been noted well before the war broke out, but it was after his liberation that he developed what would become his acclaimed approach to psychological healing, Logotherapy.

Not surprisingly, Frankl's time in captivity informed his practice and his research for the rest of his life. In those camps, in the most dire of conditions, Frankl had experienced an epiphany of sorts: he realised it was his love for his wife that made his life worth living, and that made it worth surviving his current circumstances.

The crux of his findings, from his own experience and from years of studying people's responses to struggle, centred on this: when we find meaning in an experience, we can overcome it.

Frankl teaches us that even in the hardest, most punishing environments, we have the power to survive. Once we identify meaning in an event, our resolve strengthens, and we have the will to overcome anything.

We'll look closer at the importance of meaning in your mindset for business in Chapter 3, but for now, I really want you to understand the notion that we have the capacity to choose how we respond to life, and that gives us power. Because isn't that the ultimate freedom? A freedom that we strive to find in business, and then need to fight to keep.

In Frankl's words: *"Human freedom is not a freedom **from**, but a freedom **to**."*

Frankl knew that his true freedom was the power to choose his own attitude. Even in the midst of dehumanising and atrocious conditions, his life still had meaning and his suffering had a purpose.

This is an important concept to grasp, because business will test you daily. You'll put everything you have into your business: your money, your time, your energy. You'll make personal sacrifices with no guarantees of success.

You need the strength to persevere where others quit, to wake up again and again every morning with the conviction that you'll prosper and thrive, even — or especially — when everything goes wrong.

You'll need that inner certainty even if everyone who came with you and supported you wants to turn back when the going gets tough — because it will get tough, and it's your conviction that will help you weather those storms — even when it's just you captaining your ship.

When you hit the low points in business, you need to maintain that determination, grit, and willpower to keep going, to keep your dream alive and make the choice to fight for your business — and your life for that matter — on your own terms.

Your choice is your power

Here's a question: if, like Frankl, we can choose how we perceive our circumstances, can that, in turn, make our circumstances change?

Can we change our reality, just by the way we look at it?

Or is that way too spiritual, too redolent of tie-dye and dream catchers?

What if I told you there's researched and proven science to back it up?

It's true: experiments have been conducted, even on the subatomic level, that show that electrons behave differently when they're observed. Electrons which only ever behave as particles also become waves when they're not being watched. In fact, they *only* become waves when they're not being watched.

The very act of watching changes the outcome of the reality.

We won't go too far into quantum physics here, but if you're interested, Google "The Double Split Experiment." It'll expand your mind!

For us, here and now, the takeaway is that even when we suffer injustice, feel hurt, or find ourselves in difficult situations — we have power. The power to change our mindset. To focus on how we get up, not how we got knocked down. Because the lessons that usually help us grow, test us first.

I love this story about the U.S. Marine general "Chesty" Puller. In Korea in the 1950s, while withdrawing in snow against large Chinese forces, a panicked private is said to have run up to Puller, shouting, "General! General! The Chinese have got us surrounded!"

Puller fixed the soldier with a determined stare and said, "Then we can shoot any way we want."

It's a wonderfully simple example of finding the best in a bad situation, and I'm sure his resilient and spirited attitude would have been bolstered his men.

When you can't change a situation, change how you respond to it

I'm going to bring us back to the realm of business now by offering some practical perspectives and tools for those occasions when things occur that are out of your control.

If there's one thing you definitely can't control, it's the actions and attitudes of other people. And no matter what the focus of your business is, you will, at some point, face difficult or problematic people in the form of customers or clients.

Usually you'll encounter them in the early days while you're building your brand and your reputation, and — if I'm being honest — before you develop the sixth sense required to sniff the leeches out!

Leeches… does that seem a little harsh? Maybe. Of course, I value and respect my customers, and I urge you to do the same; it just helps when they value and respect you and your business, too.

Difficult customers can (and will, if you're not prepared) suck your business dry.

What do I mean by difficult people? How bad can it get? Let me illustrate my point.

A few years ago, when I was hoping to expand into a new market, I won a decent-sized contract to build an office block in the bustling city of Sydney. That's one of my businesses: Savil Construction specialises in high quality construction and remediation work.

Essentially, the issue was this: the client wanted a Rolls Royce product for a box car price. He had very unrealistic expectations of what a project such as his would cost and was relatively clueless on what the construction process would involve. This is something I should have sniffed out very early in the relationship by using some of the sales processes and qualifying tools that we now have in place; this ensures that we pass over customers who are not a good fit with our values.

I believed, and I still do to this day, that we should always strive to please our customers and clients and endeavour to meet their needs – so I'm confident that we did our best in this situation.

This guy wasted a lot of time, both mine and the contractors I work with, by demanding never-ending changes to the works — then by refusing to pay for the changes he had requested. He was almost always unavailable when we needed him to make key decisions to keep the project going forward, and, as a result, the work was often held up. Further to that, he didn't want to accept any extensions of time caused by his lack of communication or indecision.

Worst of all, when he did pay, he was paying accounts up to six months late and often only paid a portion of what was owed. This put a huge financial strain on the business, and on me personally. Now do you see why that word leech might be appropriate?

Relations were bad, really bad, and on the verge of getting a lot worse.

How could I control the situation and stop it from escalating?

I had to take a breath, take a step back, and look at the bigger picture.

This was a complicated long-term project. A lot of stakeholders and decision makers were involved. I knew, of course, how important communication was to the whole thing, but the main learning point for me came with the realisation that diplomacy was the key to that communication.

Diplomacy enabled the project to find its feet again, to run well, and for everyone to come out alive.

Diplomacy in times of war and peace

Diplomatic communication is about saying what you mean and what you need without offending or demeaning the person you're communicating with.

Being tactful is avoiding a battle you don't want, or need, right now. And as former UK Prime Minister

Winston Churchill once said: "Tact is the ability to tell someone to go to hell in such a way that they look forward to the trip."

It requires you to keep your cool and aim for flexibility and understanding. Being open to negotiation is important, while also being realistic: keep in mind what you need to communicate and do it as clearly as possible.

For diplomacy to work, emotion has to be off the table. As irritated, offended, and frustrated as I was by my client's antagonism, I had to limit the emotional response I was having both internally and outwardly.

From there, additional, direct, and effective communication with the client became paramount to the success of the whole project. In this particular case, the client needed a big side helping of hand-holding and a whole lot of babysitting. Annoying and a drain on resources, but essential.

I soon realised my goal was quite straightforward: to get the client to the place where he understood that yes, we could deliver everything he wanted, but that there was a cost involved — in terms of both finances and time.

When he made a demand or request that fell out of the parameters of the contract, I'd start by responding with a positive: "Yes, we can do that for you…" followed by the realism, "and it will cost this amount of money and take this number of weeks."

If I didn't have the answers he wanted in that moment, I'd tell him I'd look into his request and get back to him with a quote.

As you'd expect, these meetings could last a long time and required a fair amount of preparation beforehand. We wanted to create clarity and help our customer with the misunderstanding they faced between their perception of what "should be" and the reality of "what is." But this only works with genuine customers, which most people are. A charlatan, on the other hand, still requires a strong diplomatic approach but with a clear line in the sand. If you can, as Napoleon said, aim to "conceal your iron fist in a velvet glove."

The client would still try his luck and ask why it couldn't just be done quickly and for no cost, but I would, diplomatically, stick to my guns. This additional communication was time-consuming and resource-sapping — but totally necessary.

Benefits of diplomatic communication — and how to achieve it

Diplomacy gets you closer to peace and further away from war, and, in business, it's a crucial tool in your arsenal.

Think of diplomats at peace talks: usually, there are two or more representatives from each country, all with their own agendas, all with their own ideologies to uphold, and their own constitutions to adhere to. They walk a line between talking and listening, between reflecting and asserting.

In business, diplomatic communication can achieve some or all of the following:

- It improves day-to-day communication as well as the relationship on the whole — and

that's particularly necessary for long-term projects and for B2B customers.
- It shows you're flexible and prepared to work with the client to achieve their vision.
- It can help to bring a client around to reality if they have unrealistic expectations.
- It increases the chance of repeat business with the client.
- You're more likely to get a referral or recommendation.
- It acknowledges emotions but encourages pragmatism and logic — therefore, there's less emotional drain on you.

For me, two key ingredients helped me to hone my diplomatic skills:

1. I worked on validating emotion and then taking it out of the situation: in essence, I became less sensitive to other people's attitudes and behaviour and learnt effective and realistic techniques to take things less personally as well as techniques in validating and defusing others' emotions so that we could move forward and avoid stalemates.

This simplified the whole process for me: it was business. A client's unrealistic expectations are not a criticism of your quality or a slight on your honour. Leeches are leeches and they just do what they do. To get a different outcome, you have to guide your client into the light of realism. Sounds obvious, I know — but when your business is also your dream, your passion, and one of the reasons you get up in the morning, it can be hard to detach. I learnt that a certain amount of detachment is helpful and healthy.

2. I shifted my perspective: I fully realised that I had no control how this or any client behaved. The only thing I had control over was how I responded to their behaviour.

This was incredibly empowering: I had a choice in how I looked at a situation. This was my Viktor Frankl moment, if you like.

From there, I wholeheartedly embraced diplomacy — it became a key ingredient in how I saw myself as a business owner, and it was a skill I was proud to develop.

This experience allowed me to step more into who I am as a leader. Handling difficult situations and finding a way through became exhilarating rather than frustrating and draining. I had a clearer sense of what my role was, and I understood that dealing with difficult people was part of that.

In short: I stepped up. I embraced challenging situations and I actually got excited about handling them well.

What had been a problematic and initially stressful project taught me so much and led to a real and tangible reduction in stress. A lot of business owners, including myself, during the first few years and during times of growth, carry a lot of stress. Stress plays havoc with your emotions, saps your energy, and reduces your ability to deal effectively with difficult situations.

Moreover, it weakens your relationship with your customers, and the reality is that the relationship you have with your customers is tantamount to your success.

I'll summarise this chapter with some general tips for dealing with difficult situations and customers, to keep you focused, healthy, and in a position of power: remember — you have the power to choose how you respond to any situation.

- Take a breath and take a moment for yourself and avoid knee-jerk reactions.
- Check in with yourself emotionally: are you being subjective or objective in your reaction? Objectivity can be hard to achieve when it's your money and business on the line. These questions can help achieve a broader perspective: "How much of this will matter in six months?" And, "How does this fit into the 20- or 30-year operation of my business?" Also, "How will increasing my skill in dealing with this situation make me a better business person and a better leader?"
- Remember we're all human: your client (probably!) isn't deliberately trying to make your life difficult; is it possible there's a misunderstanding? Ask questions to increase your understanding of what they want from you and the situation, and keep communication open.

- As challenging as this may seem right now, be confident that you're learning something, even — or especially — when things appear to go wrong.

All business owners learn by doing, and that takes time and consistent exposure to the industry you're in.

However, it's possible and prudent to skill yourself up with the tools for dealing with difficult customers and situations. If the discussion in this chapter has struck a chord with you, and you want to increase your skills in this area, I recommend you seek out personalised workshops and training to develop your diplomacy skills. We helped a B2B clients sales team recently with developing a system of weeding out the genuine customers from the tyre kickers and especially avoiding the charlatans, saving the company a heap of time, effort, and hundreds of dollars in easily avoidable headaches.

Training – from the right places – is a great way to put into practice what others have learnt the hard way. It increases your chances of survival and growth, while also minimising frustrating and very costly mistakes.

Let's give Frankl the last word:

"Everything can be taken from us but one thing: the last of the human **freedoms** – the power to choose your own attitude, to choose your own way."

Chapter 2 -
I: INSPIRE

It's an age-old problem: you have an idea for an innovative product, or a service that you know fills a gap in the market, and all of your instincts and intuitions tell you it's an awesome idea, it'll definitely sell, people are gonna love it.

So how do you convince everyone else you're right?

How do you translate how amazing it looks from your head into theirs?

How do you get someone — anyone — to join you on your journey — either to work alongside you, to hire you, or to buy from you?

Essentially: How do you inspire people to believe in you?

To get us close to an answer, I'd first like you to take a moment to look over your life and think about someone who has inspired you along the way.

It might have been a high school teacher, a college professor, a local entrepreneur, a celebrity, a manager or mentor, a family friend — just someone you looked at and thought: *I like what they're doing, and I like their energy.*

Picture them for a moment.

Imagine them standing in front of you: take in their posture, their facial expression. The way they carry themselves.

I'd be willing to bet that they are standing in an open position, that they look relaxed, and that they're smiling. If not smiling, they look at ease, and comfortable, and, in a word: confident.

The truth is, we're drawn to confidence. When we're in the presence of someone who radiates confidence — and I do think *radiates* is the right word — we feel a couple of different things.

We might feel a little in awe, especially if we're not so confident ourselves.

We usually feel safe, because we know we're in good hands.

And we feel inspired: a person who is effortlessly confident has the capacity to bring that out in others.

It's never about being the loudest person or the most intimidating. The most confident person can actually be the quietest in the room. Why is that? Because they don't have to try, and they have nothing to prove. Usually, you'll still see people flocking around them. Like I said, we're drawn to confidence.

Flick the switch

Confidence in yourself, and in your business, is essential if you want to inspire others to come with you. If we're talking guerrilla tactics, you're the general of your army, and your soldiers need to know they're on the winning side.

So, what do you do if you don't feel confident? What if it's always been a struggle for you?

Do you just flick the confidence switch to ON?

Well, in a way — yes!

Research has shown that confidence isn't fixed. It's not like eye colour, it's not like hair colour. Being confident is a choice we make, and we can choose to make or unmake that choice at any stage of our lives.

I'll explore some ways you can do that in a page or two, but for now, I have another reflective question for you.

Think of a time when you felt really confident about something. Anything at all. How you looked on a certain day, how you led a meeting, how you gave some great advice to your sister, how funny your Facebook status was.

Just something that you knew you'd done well.

Why did you feel confident about that thing? Did someone compliment you, or give you positive feedback?

Did you get the outcome you wanted?

Because often, our confidence is rooted in external factors, like receiving praise or seeing the results that affirm we're doing well.

So, here's the key: what happens when you're not receiving those things?

How can you radiate confidence about you, or about that awesome business idea you have, when you haven't had the external proof, or go-ahead, or the nod that allows your confidence to flourish?

In short: How do you flick that confidence switch to ON?

Acting "as-if"

You've heard that old saying, "Fake it till you make it." Well, there's a lot of truth in it!

Let me tell you a story. When I was in my twenties, I had what you might call a streak of invincibility, and it was accompanied by a willingness to apply these four words to pretty much anything: "I can do that." It actually didn't matter whether I could do a thing or not!

Picture this. It's 1997 and I'm 21 years old. I walk into a nightclub to say hi to my friend who works on the bar, and, despite having zero experience in the industry, I walk out of that nightclub with the manager's job.

How? Because when I overheard the owner saying he'd just fired the current manager for stealing cash from the register and he needed someone new to run the club, I piped up: "I can do that." Those four big little words.

"I can run the club for you," I said, "I haven't done it in a while, but I've got heaps of experience."

Talk about confident!

We exchanged a bit of banter, and I backed myself with each sentence.

"Great!" he said, "You can start tomorrow."

I had less than 24 hours to prepare for a managerial job I had absolutely no experience in. I did all I could to get in the zone: I watched Tom Cruise in *Cocktail*, bleached my hair peroxide blonde and threw on a pair of tight black jeans paired with a shiny black top. I was ready! (Forgive me; it was the early 90s)

And once I was there, I *acted* like I knew what I was doing, and I did it really really quickly: that was my method. I went at 100 miles per hour behind the bar. At the end of the night, the owner said that although he could tell I hadn't run a club in a while, he loved my energy. I ran the place successfully for a year and a half while also studying at Uni and running my own services business with my own small team.

Now, I'm not saying that you lie your way into a job or any situation! I was young, and, as I said — I thought I was invincible. What the story demonstrates is that with the right amount of enthusiasm and self-belief — you can do and achieve more than you might think. As Henry Ford said, "Whether you believe you can do a thing or not, you are right."

For me, the take-away point is the owner saying he *could tell I hadn't run a club for a while,* **but he loved my energy** — that's the value I brought to that particular role. I made him feel I was a good bet, a safe pair of hands for his business.

My confidence got that across more effectively than a printed resumé ever could. It's also a technique that used whenever I was contemplating starting a new venture of my own. I was convinced of my own ability to find a way and to succeed.

Mental rehearsal

Mental rehearsal is basically what it sounds like: it's when you imagine, in as much detail as you can, an event or situation that's coming up for you. You're essentially rehearsing it, without moving a muscle. And because it's all in your imagination — you can imagine it going amazingly well. That's the key.

This technique has been popular with athletes and sport psychologists for decades, with Muhammad Ali being perhaps the most famous pioneer — though he called it "Future History."

Ali would spend time intensely visualising winning his fights, and these visualisations would include great detail: manoeuvre's and counter attacks, the roar of the crowd, the referee holding up his arm, and, crucially: how all of that would feel.

Why does it work? Well, amazingly, just imagining doing a task well activates some of the same neural networks as actually doing the task well. You literally create pathways of success.

Applying it to business

Mental rehearsal is a brilliant tool that we can call on to achieve the outcomes we desire, and, in particular, we can use it to increase our confidence.

Say you have a presentation coming up. Some people get sweaty palms just thinking about speaking in front of an audience, never mind doing it. And that's the problem: they imagine it going really, really badly! You have to mentally rehearse it going really, really well.

Here's an example of how to use it. You should, of course, adapt it to suit your particular situation.

- Take a breath, close your eyes. Focus on your breathing for ten breaths, to help get you into a relaxed state.
- Now, imagine it's five minutes before you go on stage to do your presentation. You're prepared. You know you're content inside out and back to front, you're confident that you'll remember what you want to say

because you've taken the time to learn and rehearse not only the words, but the symphony. In these few minutes before you take the stage, you feel a perfect blend of excitement and confidence.

- Picture how relaxed but alert you are as you walk to the podium, how natural it is for you to look at the audience and greet them with a smile. Notice how engaged and friendly they are.
- You're about to begin your speech. You feel absolutely in control. Your body is relaxed, your mind is calm and in the zone. You take a breath, and you start to speak.
- Speaking is so easy, your words are clear, concise, and they flow effortlessly from you. You go at a pace that's right for you and your audience. You make eye contact with the audience, you connect, and you feel amazing — this is you, sharing what you love so easily, so confidently.

Okay, so I won't go through the entire thing, but notice how much detail you can generate just from a couple of minutes. Detail, along with really feeling and seeing yourself doing well, are the keys to this technique. Practice it often and see the difference it makes.

Positive self-talk

Positive self-talk is a great accompaniment to mental rehearsal. This tool is all about the dialogue you have *with* yourself *about* yourself.

Think about this for a moment. What kind of self-talk do you engage in? How critical are you of yourself? When you have something coming up that makes you feel nervous, like a sales pitch, do you tell yourself you'll do a great job, or do you remind yourself of all the times you got rejected, or sucked at selling, and convince yourself you'll do that again?

We often create the futures we fear because we put more focus and attention on bad experiences that in programming ourselves for success.

How can you expect to inspire others if the dialogue you have with yourself is all negative? People sense it; you can't hide it.

It sounds really simple and kind of a no-brainer to say that being more positive about yourself will make you feel more positive, so why is negative self-talk so common? Well, we're just really good at it!

The problem is, we don't always notice it.

If you want to inspire others to follow your vision, I recommend you start noticing. Drop the self-deprecation and start singing your own praises. You don't have to shout it from the rooftops, you don't even have to tell anyone else, just tell yourself. Notice when you do something well. Acknowledge it. Store it in your memory bank. Deposit it in your confidence tip jar.

A good friend of mine, a race car driver, once explained to me that one of the most important things new race car drivers learn is what to do when they lose control of the car and go into a spin.

Their natural reaction is to focus on the wall or other object they want to avoid.

And because their focus is on the wall, that's usually where they end up.

The thing is, just like the novice race car driver, so many people focus on where they don't want to be — and then they crash head on into that wall.

Switch your focus: aim for what and where you want to be.

Stand tall

Some really interesting research from social psychologist Amy Cuddy hit mainstream audiences a few years ago when she gave a TED Talk on the science behind our posture, and how standing and sitting in a certain way triggers changes in body chemistry.

Her findings are really useful for anyone who's had difficulty with confidence. Basically, just by adopting a high-power pose, you can increase your testosterone levels – that's your dominance hormone, and lower cortisol, which is your stress hormone.

A high-power pose is one which takes up space. It's about opening your body and taking up as much space as possible. You know how animals make themselves big when they're preparing for a fight? It's the same thing. Taking up more space equals more dominance — and your body recognises it and your hormones react accordingly.

The really interesting take-away about high-power poses is that we don't need to use them to convince others we're powerful. It's not about striding into the boardroom and sprawling out over several desks and seats. It's about using them *before* we go into a potentially stressful situation and letting the release of those hormones influence how we see ourselves, and how we feel about the situation. And that changes how we act, and that influences how others perceive us.

The more confident we are, the more clarity we have around our awesome ideas and our stellar vision. And others will see it too.

In essence, we can use a power-pose to communicate confidence *to ourselves*.

Try it. Next time you have something coming up, like an interview, or a presentation, take two minutes to yourself and stand with your legs shoulder width apart and your hands on your hips. Breathe and be in the moment.

If you're not sure how it should look — this pose has been dubbed "The Wonder Woman" by the media.

Two minutes. Give it a whirl.

Inspiring times

I have to say, I find it exciting, and kind of revolutionary, that we can manufacture confidence. Manufacture might not be quite the right word. Let's say we can develop it.

We can identify it as an ingredient we'd like more of, recognise the incredible things it can do, work on it, and then we get to see how it enriches our lives.

I love sharing my vision with others and I couldn't do it if I hadn't developed my confidence. If there's one skill in my life that really allows me to make a difference, it's the ability to share my passion, to inspire.

To create a vision, so to speak.

Because our vision excites and motivates people; our vision and leadership make our people want to get onboard and embark on an adventure with us. We give them something to aim for, something to believe in.

And while an admiral may be in charge of a warship, it is their skills as a navigator that are particularly appealing, because they know where they're going and how to get there. Many hands spring to take command of the wheel in a crisis – but experience tells us we'd rather be with someone who knows where they're going, rather than simply at what speed.

Our vision inspires our people, it gives them hope, purpose, and direction.

So, when I enter someone's world — anybody's world — I come in radiating positivity, enthusiasm, and with real passion, and I keep our focus on the destination.

I love challenging and empowering those around me, whether it's my staff or the people I work with as a business development trainer, to have the confidence to go where others won't.

Because we're all born great.

And even though life has beat the crap out of us, we keep getting back up; we don't let the bastards keep us down.

I love this quote from William James, the godfather of American psychology.

"Most people live in a very restricted circle of their potential being."

My advice: don't be like most people.

Using what or who inspires you

As much as you can be a self-made, independent, autonomous leader in business, there will always be people or organisations you look up to because you admire what they've achieved, and you get excited about the methods they used to get where they are.

Let me tell you how I built a successful business by drawing on what inspired me. Please note it also took a lot of hard work, and some time doing it wrong before I got it right.

First, I'll set the scene a little.

Now, I get really really excited about business.

I was a born entrepreneur and that spirit has stayed with me my whole life. I know you hear that a lot from someone who works in business — it's sort of a cliché. But seriously, at nine years old, I was making more money than most full-time adults, hustling car washes door to door after school and all weekend.

Can you imagine how thrilling that was for a nine-year-old? I was working for myself on my own terms as my own boss — and I loved it.

That experience laid the bedrock for one of my most fervently held beliefs: working for others is tantamount to slavery. I will always work for myself.

I knew all those years ago that my strength is as an individual and a leader, and I knew I could never be that true version of myself while working for someone else. Essentially, I'd had a taste of running my own business and what that would be and feel like, and it created a thirst in me and a desire for more.

Guerrilla Warfare for Business

During high school, I was doing kerb-side garbage removals starting at 3 a.m. each day, and while studying at university, I started a lawn mowing and services business, even employing a couple of guys to work with me. We basically did anything for anyone: lawns, laundry, deliveries, cleaning windows, clearing up dog poo — you name it, we did it.

All of this took hard work and perseverance, but I never thought of it as a real business. I was supporting myself, making money for myself, and I loved it.

And then I bought my own restaurant: a run-down pizzeria slap bang in the centre of the city.

I put all my savings, hopes, and dreams into it, but... it was a total dud.

I mean, just imagine that first morning I went to open the doors, excited and nervous at the same time. There, by the doorway, a bunch of people were gathered around. *Wow, customers?* I thought. No — these folks were not there ready to buy lunch from my awesome new pizzeria — they were arguing and getting ready to have a brawl!

I frantically tried to unlock the door, but the lock had a trick to it that I hadn't worked out yet, and before I knew it, the fight erupted behind me and I was calling an ambulance to pick up this poor guy who was lying on the concrete and bleeding.

Welcome to your new business, Dimitri!

I guess I should've researched the area a bit better before I bought into this one, right?

Well let me just say he wasn't the only one bleeding. It didn't take long to realise the restaurant was bleeding money left, right, and centre every day.

To be frank, when I walked into the restaurant on that first day, it smelt like dead pigeons. And there was this horrible taste in the air that made me think of … road kill.

Talk about a bad omen!

What had I done? Why did buy this place?

And what could I do to make it work?

What was the trick that would unlock that door?

In the months to come, I basically lived on a fold-out bed in the storeroom, trying to make the place work by opening longer and longer hours. I kept telling myself I just had to keep it going and keep my eyes and ears open to find a way to make it work.

I made just about every possible mistake a first-time business owner could make. I was overspending, I was undercapitalised, and I was haemorrhaging money every week.

Some sort of penny dropped when I noticed that we were busier late at night than we were during the day. The problem, however, was that we weren't set up to properly capture the late-night market. The late-night crowd expected instant service and speed, and we were designed to be the kind of restaurant where people took their time to enjoy really good quality food.

I took a risk. I made the decision to close the restaurant during the day, and only open at night. But we needed a refit first: one that allowed us to deliver to that late-night crowd with maximum speed and efficiency.

When we reopened, our focus was narrow and clear: we sold pizza by the slice to the late-night party crowd. It was a far cry from the fancy restaurant I'd hoped for, but you know the old saying, "If you're given lemons, make lemonade."

I'd been inspired by two things, and I drew on these inspirations to make that bold move. Firstly, there was MacDonald's, which temporarily closed their restaurants in the 1950s and reopened with a super condensed menu to offer speed, delivery, and consistency. In other words — good fast food.

I've always held MacDonald's in high esteem for the way they've kept efficiency central to everything they do. Even now, as a huge company with massive budgets, they still have the efficiency and effectiveness of a well-run small business, this has allowed them to dominate not only fast food but also real estate, as vertically integrating almost every segment they touch, they're on the pulse and they've maintained a real guerrilla warfare survival instinct that's kept them lean, adaptable, and responsive to their markets. I really like that.

My other inspiration came from the New York pizza places I'd seen on TV and in the movies. In

Canberra in the 90s they were unheard of — no one was doing that here, until I did it.

We were the first pizza-by-the-slice venue in our city and we made a killing. Everyone had heaps of fun — customers and staff alike. We created a party atmosphere, loud pumping music all night, and kept everything informal and fun. The staff had all the free food, beer and Red Bull they could stomach, and the whole atmosphere was fun and enjoyable.

Thus, our resilience, determination and ability to adapt had paid off.

Remember that streak of invincibility I talked about earlier? Now it was turbo-charged. My ego went through the roof: I'd made a success out of a place that I had overpaid for and smelled like roadkill. I was King of the World (or Canberra), I was Midas. Everything I touched would turn to gold, right?

Wrong.

But more on that in the next chapter.

Chapter 3 -
G: GROW

Every businessperson I know, myself included, harbours a natural and inbuilt desire to grow and to move forward. Even when we don't know exactly how to make that happen, that desire is there. We want to reach, try new things, and innovate. I'd argue that this drive is essential for our success.

But how does growth, of any kind, occur? Does it occur when we're passive, or dismissive? Or does it come when we take a risk, step into the unknown, not always knowing what the second step will be but taking that first step all the same?

The answer is: *it's always about action.*

Whether your desire for growth comes from the fact that your business is peaking (or flattening out) and needs an injection of energy, or because it's fallen on hard times and you need to work your way forward — the underpinning lesson is the same: keep moving, always.

To keep moving and to sustain momentum, you need to be open to change. Always keep in mind that you have the power to choose and control your destiny.

I've distilled my years of experience into Three Foundations for Growth which I'd like to share with you now. I invite you to explore them, get to know them, and use them as your springboard for change.

Later in the chapter, I'll share how I used them to rebuild myself after a particularly spectacular fall.

The thing is, even though we don't seek the painful experiences that forge our identities, by overcoming those challenges, we create who we are.

Life may be limited in years, but our potential to grow is limitless.

The Three Foundations for Growth: Mindset, Values, and Meaning

Mindset

Mindset has to be your number one foundation. In your guerrilla warfare arsenal, it's your most valuable weapon.

When things are tough, take a moment to check in with yourself. What's your attitude? How are you looking at your current situation?

Do you have the spirit and persistence to see challenging times through?

Are you prepared to jump into a pair of boots that are too big for you and just take the "clumsy steps" until you grow into them?

Here's the thing: fortune favours those who act, those who *do*.

But it's not about rushing in, guns blazing, yelling "Here I am!" so loud that you can't access the wider picture.

It's about balance, light and dark, yin and yang.

In addition to argument, you need exploration.

In addition to critical thinking, you need creative and constructive thinking.

In addition to logic, you need perception.

Perception is the basis of wisdom, and contrary to what many people like to believe, their emotions, feelings and intuition play a central role in thinking. Oftentimes, people's emotions make their choices and decisions.

Knowing this gives you the power to keep your emotions in check, and to view them from a broader perspective.

The importance of an innovative mindset

As a small business leader, you might be the underdog, but you have a lot going for you! You're passionate about what you do, you're able to connect with your customers, and they love your personal approach. Moreover, you're constantly learning and evolving and that means you operate in a dynamic and innovative way.

Innovation is key, and often historical guerrilla tactics in wartime have been rooted in progressive thinking and strides forward in technology.

When, in 1954, the Vietnamese dismantled their artillery to carry it up the mountains at Dien Bien Phu, they took their French opponents by surprise and utterly defeated them. Why? The French had considered such a move impossible. Their overconfidence left them weak.

A business example of a comparable situation is, arguably, the fall of the Kodak camera company. Kodak had established worldwide dominance in selling cameras and processing film to produce photographs. Although they recognised the start of digital cameras, they largely ignored this on the basis that "film is the proven way to take photos and create memories".

It didn't take long for several technological advances to combine and make digital photography the dominant way to take photos: no film or processing cost, ever-larger camera memory storage and the ability to print at home.

Overnight, Kodak became redundant. Its film processing business model collapsed, and film cameras were bought only by specialist photographers. In failing to innovate and move with the times, Kodak was left behind.

Values

In times of crisis, it's useful to consider and return to your business values: those principles that are central to what you do. Your values govern how you lead your business, whether you're just starting up or whether, like me — you're several decades in.

Within the Savil business group, integrity, honesty, and fairness are at the heart of what we do. We're passionate about excellence and doing our work right the first time because we know our reputation depends on how we deliver value — not just to our customers, but in the eyes of every member of the communities in which we work.

This is just a window into what drives us, ethically, but I wanted to share that to demonstrate that your values and principles direct you if you lose track of where you're headed.

You can veer off course when business is stagnating or when you're in crisis, and knowing what your values are can get you back on course.

In essence: *to grow, you need to go back to your roots.*

If you haven't already explored and examined this, I recommend you take some time to work out what your core business values are.

Here are some considerations to get you started on getting clear on your business values:

- What matters more to your business than making a quick buck?
- What makes your company stand out from your competitors?
- What do you stand for: as a company and, personally, as a business owner and leader?
- What would you really like to hear your staff saying about working with you?
- What would you really like to hear your customers say about your service or product?

If you have a team working with or for you, you might want to brainstorm your company values together.

Having your people on board and singing from the same song sheet is essential to your success, so even if you don't collaborate to define your values, you should definitely share what you come up with.

Beyond that, keeping your values central to how you operate is an continuing process. Here's how I do it:

- Meetings: At Savil, we have daily short, sharp, and efficient morning pep talks and meetings for all staff, and we also have weekly meetings for key staff and managers.
- I'm present: I travel from location to location, meeting and greeting staff and customers alike.
- I'm positive: I'll always congratulate and encourage everyone on work well done, as well providing bonuses and rewards to show our appreciation for those who go above and beyond. And it's not always money that motivates people, so understanding what your people value – and hiring those who share our values – is key.
- I give continuous feedback: When staff are maintaining our values, I highlight that to keep them at the forefront of what we do.
- Regular and relevant training: From our proven and road-tested sales techniques, to technical skills, to customer communication

skills, and everything in between. I ensure that everyone understands that they're a representative of Savil, and we make customer experience and the perception of our brand a top priority. Again, it's about communicating our values.

In essence, we want to make it easy for our customers to have a good experience with us. That's at the heart of everything we do.

Taking it further: What do your people value?

Alongside getting clear on what's important to your business, it's critical that you get to know what's important to the people who work for you, because that's the key to understanding what motivates them. Your people are your soldiers, and to get the best out of them, you need to actually know who they are! Don't just see them as minions or as a mass of people doing your bidding. They're individuals with their own unique desires, ideas, and perceptions.

Think about it – think about someone you know who appreciates and values you, versus someone who doesn't. When you're around the person who values you, you're so much more likely to want to help them, even if you have to put yourself out a little, even if it costs you something, because there's a feeling of equality and reciprocal respect.

Staff who are valued will perform better than staff who aren't, it's just a basic truth of business. Sadly, not every business owner understands this, and I've seen this countless times first-hand, when I've been called in to help a business that's not performing as well as it could.

Often, it's an oversight, a result of an overworked boss who hasn't got the time to get to know his staff or sees it as an inconvenience. You'll hear this a lot: "Well, I'm paying them to do a job – that should be enough!" It's so short-sighted.

If you were a baker, and your staff were loaves of bread, then it would be the "yeast" of your wisdom, experience and encouragement that would see your people rise, and keep growing.

Value your people by understanding what *they* value, know what makes them tick. Ask who's at home while they're at work; know when their kids are playing a big soccer match and ask how it went. Ask what they like to do on their days off, what books they read, what music they like. Play that music in the office! Tell them to make a playlist. Find out what their hobbies are, what artistic interests they have.

I like this quote from Stella Adler: "Life beats down the soul, but art reminds us that we have one."

The really brilliant thing here is that if you value your staff as artistic, creative people, they're more likely to bring fresh and bright ideas to your business, and because they know you value them, they'll be much more likely to want to share their ideas with you. This boosts your business as much as or more than seeing their suggestions adopted rewards and further motivates your staff!

When people feel appreciated and "seen," when they love doing what they do, they're happy to get out of bed each morning because they know they're contributing to something great. In short: you'll have a team of loyal allies.

Meaning (and Purpose)

While your values help you return to what's important to you, it's when you find meaning in a difficult situation that you acquire the drive to keep going, keep growing, and keep fighting in tough times.

Remember this from Chapter 1? "Once we identify meaning in an event, our resolve strengthens, and we have the will to overcome anything."

I'd like to develop the idea of meaning and make it as practical for us as possible by focusing it to include the notion of purpose.

Purpose is like a lighthouse that guides us on those dark and foggy nights. It keeps us on our journey. It sees us safely through the doubt, the obstacles, and the pain along the way.

For me, I find meaning and purpose in creating new businesses and connecting great people to do what they love. Business is both my hobby and my, well… business! I love talking about business and sharing what I know with the world and those who want to grow. It's what gets my blood pumping and how I get my totally natural and addictive high.

But more deeply and personally, I find meaning in creating a better world for my kids. I always aim to show them by example that they can create their own way through life with the right mindset and the right skillset.

I tell them daily how I believe in them and know they can do anything that they set their minds to. As they're girls, instilling self-belief in them is particular important to me and my wife. So, yes, first and foremost, my purpose, my meaning, my reason for being is rooted in my family.

I feel incredibly lucky that I get to do what I love every day, and being the captain of my own ship is a key part of that. And, at the risk of flogging the metaphor, I love building new ships to sail, sharing my ship building knowledge and motivating others to build their own ships too!

Uncovering your purpose

If you accept that it's your purpose that guides you, then finding your purpose, is essential to staying on course. Your purpose doesn't have to be one single thing, and it doesn't have to be set in stone.

As your life and business develop, so might your purpose.

It's interesting to contemplate it, whether for the first time or the fiftieth.

If you want to explore this in more depth, you can use these questions as a starting point:

- What gets you out of bed every morning?
- What gets your blood pumping?
- What really satisfies you?
- When do you feel most "switched on"?
- Have you ever been so engrossed in something you forgot to eat? What were you doing at the time?
- If you knew you had one year to live, what would you spend your time doing?
- How would you like your children to remember you? Or: what would you like to have written on your gravestone?

My advice: be light and have fun with this. The answers might not come right away, but if you can just start getting your head around the idea that your purpose can guide you through a bad or challenging situation, you'll be better prepared.

And, crucially, when you ride the waves of a disaster you'll come out the other side a stronger, more focused version of yourself.

In short: you will have grown, changed, and evolved — and if you prize those qualities, your business too can grow, change, and evolve.

When the going got tough

I'd like to pick up where I left off at the close of Chapter 2. I've mentioned a couple of times how I've had my fair share of business highs and lows — it's time now to tell you how I used the three foundations for growth: **Mindset, Values and Meaning**, to get through the toughest period in my business, and in my life.

It's 2008, I'm 31 years old, and I have it all: a lovely wife, a beautiful family, and several thriving businesses.

At this time, my efforts were all on expansion: I was investing heavily in property development and new construction projects.

Remember the pizza place? That little gold mine that I'd nurtured and raised to be a roaring success? We'd expanded to four new locations now, partly to capture more market share, but mostly to protect market share from the new competitors swooping in. I was halfway through converting it into a 1920s prohibition-style speakeasy nightclub. It would be stylish, classy and chic — and, though I didn't yet know it, it would make nowhere near as much money as selling pizza by the slice.

Truth is, I was in my early thirties, incredibly ambitious, driven, and full of ideas — but I was in debt up to my ears. To top it all off, I borrowed today's equivalent of a million dollars to invest in one single speculative mining company.

One. Single. Company.

A million dollars.

What could go wrong? I thought. It was a strong company. Yeah, it was kind of risky — but so far, all of my business risks had paid off. I was Midas, remember? The same man, the same touch.

At that time, everyone was investing in mining; there was a huge mining boom in Australia, and I was sure I'd invested well.

I truly believed there were only two ways the investment could go: I would either make more money, or I would break even.

How totally, completely, and utterly wrong I was.

As I said, it was 2008 — you may know what's coming next.

We were on the edge of the 2008 global financial crisis, and the very next day, to my absolute horror, the company I'd invested in released the terrible news that they weren't able to secure financing to meet the massive debts they were in.

Their value suddenly dropped by 45%, and within 24 hours of making my investment, I'd lost every cent I'd put in. Worst still, most of the money wasn't mine — it had been borrowed from the bank — and they wanted it back now, right now, or even better — yesterday.

With the onset of the GFC, finance suddenly froze on all of the construction projects I was running, and, in general, people were wary, spending less. I kept the pizza place open through the renovation, but the fact was we were losing money. Other outlets had caught on to the pizza-by-the-slice trade and what had been my goldmine was now barely covering what it cost to run it.

The day I lost a million dollars (I can say it casually now), I remember seeing a bunch of well-dressed attractive young girls walking past the pizza restaurant. It was late, approaching midnight, and, let me tell you — the later the night gets, the weirder peoples' behaviour.

One of the girls leant up against a post at the front entrance, and suddenly she squatted — and … well, what can I say — could my day get any worse? I just thought, *Yep, that sums it up: I'm basically pissing it all away.*

Virtually overnight, I'd gone from being on top of the world, to less than zero. I lost my businesses, I had to sell my properties, and I could've been forced into bankruptcy if I hadn't mustered the will to fight, to survive.

But I held on; I held on. Why?

By this point in my career, my **mindset** was focused and clear, despite my situation. I've always had a fighter's mindset and it was time to really test and use it.

I returned to my business **values**, and my personal values. Small business isn't just about money: it's about the people who work with you and have helped you along the way, and I had a lot of people with me, depending on me. My values were rooted in community, honour, and self-respect. I needed to hold my head up high and keep going.

But there was more than this huge upheaval threatening to throw me off course. Alongside my professional struggles, my wife had just given birth to our first daughter, and it was a traumatic, wrenching, gruelling and dangerous time for all of us.

Born three months early, my little girl weighed just over two pounds and spent the first months of her life in intensive care. It was the toughest experience of my life. I was sleeping at the hospital then going into work the next day, exhausted, scared – but not beaten.

I had to stay strong for my family. I had to look forward, I had to keep moving forward.

I fortified myself for my wife, drew on everything I had to stay standing and to get our daughter through this time.

In terms of the business, I told my people that I'd understand if they moved on to greener pastures. Amazingly, most of my people stuck with me.

After ten weeks in intensive care our little fighter was allowed home, and I threw myself into learning everything about her. I knew that my family gave my life meaning, and that had expanded, deepened, and intensified with her arrival – and would expand even further when my second daughter was born four years later.

In terms of the business, my saving grace came when I won a contract to construct a multimillion-dollar commercial building for one of Australia's largest companies. I had no idea what I was in for. I mean I'd built houses, but this was a seriously complicated commercial structure.

My back was to the wall, but I used this to motivate me. I knew that not only was I great at working stuff out under pressure, but that I could find, build, motivate, and lead the right people and the right team to get that project done. The result was that it strengthened us in dozens if not hundreds of ways and launched our company to the next level.

Surviving this time made me realise I'd earned my stripes, well and truly, and it's one of the driving forces for the development of my business coaching and facilitating. I get a genuine kick out of sharing my story and everything I've learnt with others.

Ten years on I'm the proud owner and CEO of a commercial construction company that has employed more than 300 local staff and contractors over the years. I paid off all my debts, got our home back, and kept my reputation intact.

I rode the waves, captained the ship, and now take pride in being an anchor for those who work with me, as well as a beacon for those who attend my workshops and presentations.

There's an old quote by Vince Lombardi, a legendary American football coach that fits perfectly here: "It's not whether you get knocked down; it's whether you get back up that counts."

Nowadays, I prefer an Aussie quote coined by Tom, a close friend of mine who's also survived his fair share of business battles and successes. He said, "Dimitri, don't let the bastards keep you down; get up, stay up, and keep going."

Chapter 4 -
H: HERO

Rewriting the hero narrative

If you look up the word *hero* in the dictionary or online, you'll get definitions that include phrases such as, "a person admired for their outstanding achievements," and "someone displaying exceptional courage or bravery." Examples of the word in use throw up terms such as, "war hero", "national hero", and then of course there's the colloquialism "from zero to hero."

All of these definitions suggest that acting heroically happens suddenly and on a huge scale, and while that's *one* way of looking at heroism, I'd argue that being a hero isn't measured by how big or attention-grabbing the act itself is, but by the courageous mindset and attitude of the individual.

The thing is, heroism a long-term mindset. Having a hero's mindset is not something you decide one day and decide against the next. It's a choice you make about how you live as a member of society, and, in our case — as a business leader.

In business, being a hero is about having the courage to stand up for what you believe in, and the people you believe in. In doing that, you become an inspiration for your team and for the wider community.

Being a hero can be demonstrated in a multitude of ways. It can be about helping someone who's struggling, and that could be with a physically heavy load or a metaphorically heavy load. It can be about supporting someone who's experiencing injustice — on any level. Often, being a hero is about being kind when the world is not.

Let's redefine the notion of what a hero is and embrace our inner hero: that spark within almost all business-minded people, which is set alight by our vision to build and innovate great products and services and to improve the lives of those we work with and for.

Hero might be a daunting word, but don't be intimidated by it. I'm not suggesting we all wear capes and scale skyscrapers, rather, that we adopt a hero mindset, taking a self-assured, confident, and courageous stance in how we do business.

If that sounds out of line with guerrilla warfare tactics, then forgive me, but you've missed the point: having a hero mindset is a crucial part of your weaponry.

Let's look at how we can incorporate this mindset into how we run our businesses, and our lives.

Leading your army

Don't just be a manager: be a leader. Leading people is about getting the best out of your team individually and collectively. It's about recognising their strengths, empowering each member, inspiring them, and nurturing them. There are no quick fixes for this — it's a way of being, a way of seeing the people who work for you.

Savil has helped countless business owners in this area and have found that it often comes down to the same thing: managers expect a certain standard from their staff (and get frustrated when it's not delivered), but unknown to them, they're sending all the wrong messages and failing to support their staff in quite straightforward ways.

We helped one company in particular who was having a really hard time motivating its staff. We discovered relatively quickly that there were key areas where they could support their staff more, and, in turn increase their motivations — areas such as carrying out appraisals, having incentives for sales, and improving their overall methods of communication.

But it wasn't until we ran some workshops with the manager that we got to the crux of it: on the one hand, this guy was a good manager, hardworking, and dedicated, the kind who had built his business from the ground up. The issue was that he was a perfectionist, and it was this unrealistic expectation that was holding his business back — not his "lacklustre team".

The manager had unrealistic expectations of what his staff could and would deliver, and worse than that — if he thought someone was doing substandard work, he took over the situation (most likely seething with frustration) and did whatever task it was himself. This created a difficult atmosphere of mistrust, and when we uncovered that, it was suddenly obvious why his staff weren't motivated.

We worked with the manager and the whole team to build that essential trust required between leaders and their people. Remember, in guerrilla warfare for business your staff is your army – and when it's behind you, you're unstoppable.

As a heroic business leader:

- See your staff as equal to you.
- Never ask a staff member to do something that you wouldn't do yourself. But don't do it for them
- Don't try to be right all the time — listen and be prepared to learn from your team.
- Don't try to be perfect — it's okay to not have all the answers, and to show vulnerability.
- If you mess up, hold up your hands and take responsibility. This encourages your team members to highlight their (OR, "any") mistakes before they affect your firm's reputation.
- Recognise the natural talents of the people who work for you.

- If you sense a staff member needs encouragement in a particular area, offer extra support or training if appropriate.

Getting the best from your army

One of the realities of being a good leader is being able to marry what you expect from your people against what they can actually deliver.

Usually, what a person can deliver is dependent on their resources, physical and mental. A good leader knows how to nurture and bring out the best in their staff. Often, our skill comes in working with what we've got — and sometimes, what we've got is someone who can't do what you need them to do at a particular time.

With experience, you get more savvy and shrewd at recognising whether a person working for you can deliver what you need. Through trial and error and working with diverse people, you learn how to enlist and hire smartly and manage individuals with all their quirks, needs, shortcomings, and talents.

Ultimately, you might need to let a person go if you can't develop them further or if you simply don't have the capacity for them within your business.

The last thing you want to do is to put pressure on someone to do a job that's not for them. They get unhappy, you get unhappy, and it's a downward spiral from there.

This is an area where a lot of business owners struggle, and it's an area where we're often brought in to help. We work with managers to find ways to use the skills of their workforce and get really awesome and discerning about choosing new staff, as well as developing existing staff. The aim is always to put people in positions where they shine and, importantly, where they can actually maximise their value to a business.

In short, it's pretty hard to use a hammer to saw a piece of wood.

You can't force someone to do something they aren't skilled or suited to, no matter how much you want to. Einstein said it best: "Everyone is a genius. But if you judge a fish by its ability to climb a tree, it will live its whole life believing that it is stupid."

Stand up for those who can't stand up for themselves

If I had a brand at high school, it was this. I was known for standing up for the "weaker" kids by directly confronting the bullies, and I took this a step further by encouraging and empowering those so-called weak kids to find the strength and confidence to stand up for themselves.

Truth is, my high school was rough. I've already talked about the bullying I faced and how I dealt with it, and maybe that's why I was always the first to speak up when I saw anything that resembled injustice, even when it involved a teacher not doing their job right.

But my focus was always those kids who didn't have a voice or the courage to fight back. I wanted to show them that they didn't have to put up with tyranny or bullying of any kind. It didn't have to be a fact of life for them.

The worst case of this happened when we were at camp, and the Alpha male boys made a target out of a really nice kid, Gus, who was Iraqi. It was the time of the first Kuwait invasion, and Gus was taunted with racist slurs — but that was just the tip of the iceberg. The bullies encouraged him to take part in a rappelling activity at school camp, and even though Gus was terrified, he did it — thinking he'd get some respect. How wrong he was.

Once he was over the edge of the mountain, the guys at the bottom started hurling not just insults at him, but rocks too. Actual rocks. Gus froze with fear and couldn't move, and I couldn't not intervene.

First, I took care of the ring leader with a couple of swift punches. Next, I encouraged Gus down the mountain, making sure he was okay as he landed. He was very obviously shaken and distressed.

Once we were back at school I took Gus under my wing and coached him to have the confidence and skills to fight back next time he was attacked. And he did — and I was so proud, because I knew how scared he was, and I knew what it took. Once he was no longer an easy target, the bullies backed off considerably.

The take-away "hero" moment from this is not about throwing punches: it's about standing side by side with people who need you and showing them how to get through the bad times and be the best version of who they can be.

I recommend you look out for the people in your team who are quiet and be patient with those who seem shy. There doesn't have to be an obvious incident like the one with Gus; a good business leader is intuitive and spends time observing and understanding their staff. If you sense someone is struggling, ask if you can help. Even just asking how someone is can make a huge difference to their day. Take care of those who work for you and they'll take care of you and your business.

Morale

It's essential to keep your staff motivated and to make sure they know you believe in them. Take a leaf out of Napoleon's book: he'd keep his elite troops, especially the Old Guard, in full view of his enemy. Those enemy generals, knowing they were barely holding off Napoleon's *regular* battalions, would begin to tremble when they saw the Guard advance. Their defeat was surely approaching, and because they believed it, defeat became a self-fulfilling prophecy.

Don't make money your number one priority (when you can)

Once your business is financially secure, you might make the decision to take on work that you don't get paid for — at least not in the financial sense of the word.

One of my proudest professional moments came when I ran a pro-bono project to build a playground at my daughter's school. I called on every favour owed to me and a hundred more besides. By this time in my career, I was established and experienced in the construction trade and people were willing to help me because they knew me, because it was a community project, and the people I work with are community oriented and knew they could trust me.

The project was one of the most rewarding of my career, and the fact that both my daughters spend time every day in the playground that I built for them is important to me. Like me, they have their share of difficult moments with bullies at school, and building the playground, with its emphasis on peace and relaxation, was my way of fighting for them in the right way and in a way they can learn from. That's less about being a hero, and more about being a dad.

If there are any heroes in the equation, it's my two girls: for learning so much and trying to better themselves all the time. They are much better with this than their dad was at the same age. They have their own personal struggles and are constantly learning to apply all the new techniques they are introduced to and incorporating all of this with the understandings of life they are developing. Even though others can be cruel and quick to try to knock you down socially, they get back up, and they care for each other and look out for each other. Both of them are fighters; both of them are my inspiration, and they're learning all the skills to tackle life the right way. And the "right way" includes social and verbal skills that have taken me a lifetime to learn and pass on.

A hero knows it's okay to call for back-up

Remember my mantra? *If you fight, you might lose, but if you don't fight — well then, you've already lost.*

Well, it can be adapted slightly to say something about the nature of asking for help. Often, we're a bit reticent to call on the expertise, knowledge, or even labour of others to help achieve our dream of running a successful business. Some see it as sign of weakness, or they have an aversion to relying on others.

This is such a limiting way of doing business and is definitely the product of a mind that's too proud! Asking for help or calling for back-up when you need it is the sign of nuanced, progressive and realistic thinking – and it's a classic guerrilla tactic. No one person can be expected to be the fount of all the good ideas. Here's the truth of it: if you ask, you might not get what you want, but if you don't ask … well then you definitely won't get it!

This applies to sales; to expectations of employees and new staff, contractors, customers, clients; and, basically, all areas of life. There's no shame in our game. Our game is business development, building, creating, and innovating, and that isn't possible unless you ask for what you want.

Ask, ask, and ask again. If that doesn't work, ask a different way, and if that doesn't work — ask the next person.

Ask often and persistently until you find the right people to join your team, to grow your business, to serve as customers and clients, to create a vision and to build your dream into reality… ASK!!!

Going above and beyond

I have an amazing friend in my life called Joseph or Joe as he prefers to be known. Joe and I have worked together for decades: he was my manager at the pizzeria and he's been my best friend since high school. I have to say, he's a bit of a hero to me.

I've witnessed Joe going above and beyond the call of duty dozens of times. It's just in his nature. I remember how he'd take pizza out to the homeless lady who sat in a doorway near our restaurant — and it wasn't the old food we couldn't sell. He'd always take her a fresh slice, and he'd take the time to talk to her as well. It was an everyday, easy, natural kindness from him, and it made a huge difference in her world.

Joe's ability to see beyond stereotypes led us to a really great but unconventional business decision when we employed a guy no one else would take a chance on: he was homeless, had schizophrenia, and couldn't speak English. He came to work for us and was one of the most loyal and best workers we ever had.

The thing is, going above and beyond isn't always about making grand statements or gestures, it's about making connections for no other reason than to help someone or influence their life — or their day — in a positive way.

Three ways for a business leader to access the hero within

Be courageous

In small business, you'll take several if not dozens of hits. Be prepared and be willing to absorb them! If you fall down, get back up. With a clear vision, you can take anything because you understand it's all part of your journey. When things get tough, remind yourself what matters to you personally, maintain your long-term focus, and don't allow what others think to deter you from pushing forward. Get up and keep going, and lead the way, even if no one is following yet.

Don't be afraid to ask for help if you need it. Sometimes being brave is about saying you need a hand.

Just like confidence, courage is a skill you can develop. We'll build on this in the following chapter with a closer look at confronting the fear of failure.

Be an independent thinker

Be willing to go against the crowd and challenge the status quo. It might mean standing alone for a while — so be okay with that. Know your own moral compass: what do you believe in? What, and who, are you prepared to stand against? Who are you willing to support and stand *with*?

Be prepared to see it through

When you choose your path and your purpose, don't back down half way through. This doesn't mean you're so stubborn and inflexible that you can't re-evaluate what you need to move forward — but it means that you don't compromise on your dreams, and you hold your nerve.

Dimitri Livas

Chapter 5 -
T: TRUTH (and Authenticity)

This moment

What if there's no good and no bad?

No right and no wrong?

What if there's only ever this, right now, this moment? This authentic moment that we're in.

Okay, what I'm saying here might seem counterintuitive for someone so business-minded. Business is all about planning, right? Looking ahead, looking back, analysing your efforts, and strategically working out what the best next move will be.

Well, yes — there's an element of that — but I believe we can have *too much* of that.

I believe a heavy focus on strategy and planning and forecasting leads us to a place where we rely far too heavily on our minds. We obsess over what's happening next so much that we lose sight of where we are *now*.

Consider this; all business is risky, especially starting a business. Financial planners tend to advise safe options, they're risk averse by nature. Would they have started your business? Chances are – no! So just bear in mind that some, even much, of the planning "advice" you hear isn't as important to your business as the vision you have in your mind, towards which you're still advancing.

Research in the United States (at Swarthmore College, Pennsylvania) showed that excessive thinkers or ruminators are less committed to their lives. Furthermore, they lose sight of the bigger picture really easily.

In essence, overthinking makes us less alert, less aware, less intuitive — and in business, those are essential winning qualities.

Confession

I actually get really excited about this concept of the power of the present moment. I should come clean here that I have a second love: after business, or maybe alongside business, part of my heart belongs to acting. In particular, I love improvisation.

Not such a traditional business man, right?!

Here's why I love acting and storytelling.

For 100,000 years, humans have landed in trouble: sex, drugs, war, death, love… and at the end of the day, we'd gather the tribe around the campfire and tell stories. "My god, did you see what happened to Jenny today? That sabre-toothed tiger nearly took her head off!"

Today, of course, the biggest campfire is Facebook or YouTube, and there's such an appetite for drama and entertainment — which is great, because drama takes away that burden of consciousness that we carry around all day. It lets us detach from reason, and free ourselves from thinking, and from constantly having to weigh stuff up.

It's all about connection

It actually makes a lot of sense that I feel an affinity for business and improv. I love connecting with people. Whether it's on stage, in a boardroom, in a sales meeting, in an interview situation — connection is what gets my blood pumping.

And you can't connect in any moment, or any situation, if you're not IN those moments and situations!

Think about it: so many people live in the past, going over past mistakes, or past triumphs. Replaying them like an old movie in their heads.

Then there are the people who say they don't dwell on the past, they only look forwards. Is that better, somehow?

Okay, yes: knowing where you're headed, what your goals are, and where you're aiming for is important, but you can't function from there.

If you close yourself off to the moment you're in and live in the future instead, even if the future is a day away, an hour away, a moment away — you're missing out on so many opportunities and possibilities you never knew existed — the possibilities of the now. You literally disconnect from life.

And people pick up on it. It's so obvious.

I see this a lot when I'm coaching people to give great business talks and presentations. The aim for any speech is to make it engaging, insightful, and inspiring, whether you're delivering it to a packed auditorium, or a small roomful of people, or even to a single person or a camera lens.

The basis for an unforgettable speech, one that you enjoy as much as your audience, is staying in the moment. I do a lot of coaching with clients to keep them "present." I've seen it work wonders for a lot of different people with different presenting styles, from those who have zero confidence at the start to those who are too bombastic and overbearing and need to centre themselves. All find their true voice and power when they accept and engage with the present moment.

When I'm on stage giving a presentation to an audience, whether it's impromptu or scripted, there's a kind of celebration going on. I get to celebrate the audience being there, and I get to be present for the moment. I'm not thinking about tomorrow or later this afternoon. I'm there, in the moment, aware and alert. That's authenticity.

I'm certain you've seen those presenters giving a speech and you just know they're going through the motions, half there, half not. The moment they take themselves out of the present moment, the audience sees it. They might not have seen Elvis leave the building, but the audience know he sure as hell has!

So where did Elvis go? And how do we get him back?

Okay, I'll stop it with the Elvis analogy. But seriously, when you switch off, or you zone out, you forfeit so much.

Let's look at how we can keep you in the room, and in the moment.

Stop overthinking

The truth is, we have this tendency to overthink pretty much everything. I get it: in business, the stakes are high, often huge. We put our lives, our security, our health sometimes, on the line to fulfil a dream or realise an ambition. No one chooses that lightly.

So, it's little wonder that we can get ourselves stuck in our heads. We take too long to make decisions or analyse the life out of something before making a move.

Overthinking makes it all too hard. Projecting forward out of the moment makes *everything* more complicated than it needs to be.

I hate to be the one to tell you, but your brain is the demon on your shoulder. It weighs stuff up, it makes you second guess yourself, it makes you question yourself.

Am I right? Am I wrong?

You know what I am? I'm right all the time.

You know what I am? I'm wrong all the time.

I am! I am! Right here right now!

Your brain can be your greatest asset and your worst enemy. We have to know when to shut it up and just… be.

Or, more accurately when it comes to business: just do.

Knowing when to spend less time thinking, and more time doing.

Think about it this way: what could you be missing, while you're obsessing over something that's already happened, or may never happen?

Throw the inner critic out

I'd hazard a guess to say we all have one of these. It's that voice in your head that likes to pipe up, usually when you're about to try something new, or even when you're just *considering* trying something new.

"Better not do that, it won't work out, you're not dynamic enough to do that, if you do that you'll be laughing stock, you'll lose profits, you'll be less credible…" Yadda yadda yadda.

The inner critic is usually someone you know like your mother, your father, your old football coach, or that friend who's not really a friend because they have this knack of making you feel inferior… you know the type.

Whoever's voice is whispering — or yelling in your ear — they're totally taking you out of the moment.

I have one. It's my first coach. He was my role model. He guided me through my teenage years, taught me to look after myself, and instilled a fighter's spirit in me.

Because I looked up to him, I always wanted him to be impressed with everything I did. Whenever he was around I felt this intense pressure to do things well, and that intense pressure became my inner critic.

Thus, in every challenging situation, my thoughts turned to: "What would Boston think if he were here?"

Boston is highly competitive. He saw potential in me, and I worked hard to learn all the skills he passed on and wanted me to learn to be a winner. And though he was supportive, he wasn't always patient. He was strict too and had little tolerance for his own mistakes and failure, let alone mine. Although he understood that practice and mistakes are vital to learning and developing your own unique strengths, there was a subjective limit to the number of mistakes that were permitted before frustration kicked in.

Boston's is the voice that encourages me to try my best, and it's also the voice that gets disappointed when I fail. It tells me I'm strong and I can do anything, but it also tells me I'm weak if I can't live up to other people's expectations. Thankfully, I recognise it and know it's not real.

The truth is, we all fail at some point in our lives, sometimes big, sometimes small. We need to push forward and strive to succeed, and although our inner critic may help us develop some strengths, at some point, it needs to be banished in order for us to grow and develop as independent individuals.

When I was eighteen years old, I got the inkling that Boston's way of seeing the world wasn't always in line with mine.

We were both nuts about Judo and were lucky enough to attend a training camp and be coached for a short time by Alex, a world-renown coach.

Being in the room with the two of them taught me so much, just from seeing their different approaches.

Alex was extremely patient. He allowed us to learn by doing and tweaking one thing at a time.

Boston was impatient, both with me and with himself. He got upset when he made a mistake, and that frustrated him.

And the effect? Well, he got more and more worried about not making a mistake, and that made me desperate to not make any either. I couldn't focus on the moves we were practicing, I could only focus on not getting it wrong. It made me stiff, and cautious, and, drum roll ... more prone to making mistakes.

I was lost in a vicious cycle, where the only inevitable outcome was failure. Can you see how relevant that is to business? The more we strive for absolute perfection and the more intolerant we are with mistakes, the harder it is to get it right.

Striving for perfection and fearing failure are huge obstacles, and ones I'm about to address in the next part of this chapter.

I wonder if my old coach had an inner critic having a go at him in that training camp classroom?

If we're being kind about it, the inner critic has one purpose: to stop you from failing. If we're being realistic and truthful about it: if left unchecked, it's going to stop you from succeeding.

Whenever that voice pipes up, you can issue a friendly: "Thanks for your concern, but I'm doing just fine. On you go."

Face your fears until your inner critic has no power over you anymore, and it just becomes a voice — an opinion like any other.

It takes practice but start to turn the volume down on this, and, eventually, you'll turn it off altogether.

Know that it's okay to fail

Okay, this is such a big one. I'd say fear of failure is the number one inhibitor for everyone in all walks of life. It can hold us back from everything — moment by moment.

Here's the thing:

The earlier we learn that it's okay to fail, the more success we can expect.

If I could impart one piece of advice to anyone starting out in business, it's this: get comfortable with failure. And I don't means this in a cynical way, like, "You'd better get used to failure!" I mean it in a celebratory way, like, "Hey you failed! That's a sign you tried! Good for you! Let's crack open the champagne."

To a lot of people, the idea of celebrating failure is counterintuitive, but it's a great way to dispel fear around it and get a sense of freedom around choice making generally.

Improv has an awesome game called The Failure Game, in which you applaud and cheer whenever someone makes a mistake. Now, if you need a shortcut to getting okay with failure, that's it!

And you can adapt this to your everyday life. I created a game with my daughter in which we changed the rules of swing ball. Basically, we competed for who could play the *worst,* and doing so took away the stress of being perfect. We had lots of fun and laughs and she got better and better naturally without even wanting to. It was so awesome to see.

In improv, there isn't one accepted school or technique of How to Do It. You become your own school of improv, and, as there is only one you — that's a pretty exclusive school.

Here's the link to business: even though you spend your formative years becoming a crazy quilt of teachers, coaches, mentors, books you've read, and so on — you eventually become yourself.

For me, business allows me the freedom to become the only version of me, and to find my style as I develop my skills. It's a never-ending process.

It's never too late to become yourself. You can still collect best practices from those who inspire you, and you'll still load up your tool belt from wherever you can, but you'll be yourself.

When sometimes you fall into the valley of suck – make fun of yourself and do something else for a little bit. Then revisit the fundamentals and start again.

Learn by doing

It's not just in face-to-face interactions where our tendency to step out of the moment can occur. Overthinking, listening to the inner critic, and fear of failure hold us back even when we're on our own.

Imagine a writer sitting quietly in a cabin in the woods, at her desk, a warm open fireplace crackling in the background, her desk lamp shining a dim light on her notepad. She's waited for weeks for this moment: for the peace, for the time, for the space to write.

Okay, what shall I write? she thinks. And thinks. And overthinks.

You're so bad at this, says her inner critic.

She manages to turn the volume down on that voice a little, and at last settles on something she'd like to write about. Then her mind fast-forwards to the moment her editor will read her words. To how many one-star reviews she'll get. That's her fear of failure kicking in.

And she's paralysed.

She couldn't be further out of the moment.

All she needs is to just *be*… and *do*.

Unplug the cork, write — bleed even — bleed onto the page, and express what she knows.

We learn by doing. Life's not perfect. You don't walk into every situation and get it right every time. That's the beauty of it, that's how you earn your stripes.

Forget the destination

I'm sure you've heard this before, but here it is:

Life is about the journey, not the destination.

It's very much a kind of a cliché, right? And it can jar on the nerves, especially for business-minded people.

Are your hackles up? Is it too wishy-washy? Do you want to throw this book out of the window?

Stay with me… this has helped my life, and the way I do business, *so much.*

In truth: it's about balance. There's a time for planning, and a time for being.

When I'm presenting, I'm being. I'm on a journey with the audience, and, sometimes, I know where I want to end up, and, sometimes, I'm totally surprised by going in another direction.

I stay open to the moment so that I can sense what the audience wants and needs.

And that makes it interesting — for the audience and for me. We all learn, we all grow, we're all in the moment — and on that journey — together.

It makes it authentic too. You see, authenticity isn't about being factually correct, it's about a different kind of truth. It's about telling a story with emotional content, a story that's real to you.

Develop a spirit of exploration

When you know that it's okay to fail, that you don't have to be perfect, you get so much more freedom in the way your approach the world and its challenges (and opportunities). You get to play, to experiment, to try — and you feel safe while doing it.

You're like a kid who never grows up, like Peter Pan in Neverland.

What if you could just keep flying?

What if you could take other people with you on that joyous journey? What if you could make it both surprising and inevitable?

The sweet spot is that balance between knowing who you are, where you're going, and being open to the moment and to all of that changing. And not being afraid of it.

There is no good, there is no bad, there is no right, there is no wrong… there's just that moment that we're in.

Life is for living. Don't be afraid to get in there up to your elbows, get your hands dirty, and make a mess.

Take that step and keep stepping to create the life you deserve. Choose your own destiny through the unity of your ideas and purpose and by the decisions and choices you make.

CONCLUSION

Remember this: You always have the **freedom** to choose how you perceive a situation, and in that choice lies your power. **Inspire** people to believe in you and they'll follow and fight for your dream with you. Develop the right mindset for success, use it to uncover your values and your purpose and you'll see your business **grow**. Fight like a **hero**, lead your army and stand with courage in your convictions. Be a **truth** seeker: seek the truth in every moment, in every opportunity, and in every exploration and expedition.

This is your revolution. Be fearless on the frontline whether you're a lone wolf facing hostilities or a general leading an army of troops.

This is your mission, and you're in command of your success.

Know that every sacrifice leads to glory. Tool up and expand your armoury.

Hold your vision.

Keep victory in sight ... *and fight.*

Dimitri Livas

*For more information, please visit
https://www.dimitrilivas.com*

www.ingramcontent.com/pod-product-compliance
Lightning Source LLC
Chambersburg PA
CBHW050910300426
44111CB00010B/1469